# This Wedding Planner Belongs To:

♥ _____ ♥

_____

# Initial Planning Phase

## IDEAS FOR THEME

## IDEAS FOR VENUE

## IDEAS FOR COLORS

## IDEAS FOR MUSIC

## IDEAS FOR RECEPTION

## OTHER IDEAS

## Notes & Ideas

# Wedding Budget Planner

Expense MANAGER

| CATEGORY/ITEMS | BUDGET | ACTUAL COST | BALANCE |
|---|---|---|---|
| | | | |
| | | | |
| | | | |
| | | | |
| | | | |
| | | | |
| | | | |
| | | | |
| | | | |
| | | | |
| | | | |
| | | | |
| | | | |
| | | | |
| | | | |
| | | | |
| | | | |
| | | | |

# Wedding Budget Checklist

| CATEGORY | BUDGET | ACTUAL COST | DEPOSIT | BALANCE |
|---|---|---|---|---|
| | | | | |
| | | | | |
| | | | | |
| | | | | |
| | | | | |
| | | | | |
| | | | | |
| | | | | |
| | | | | |
| | | | | |
| | | | | |
| | | | | |
| | | | | |
| | | | | |
| | | | | |
| | | | | |
| | | | | |
| | | | | |
| | | | | |

# Wedding Contact List

| IMPORTANT VENDOR CONTACTS | | | | |
|---|---|---|---|---|
| | NAME | PHONE # | EMAIL | ADDRESS |
| OFFICIANT | | | | |
| RECEPTION VENUE | | | | |
| BRIDAL SHOP | | | | |
| SEAMSTRESS | | | | |
| FLORIST | | | | |
| CATERER | | | | |
| DJ/ENTERTAINMENT | | | | |
| WEDDING VENUE | | | | |
| TRANSPORTATION | | | | |
| OTHER: | | | | |
| OTHER: | | | | |
| OTHER: | | | | |
| | | | | |
| | | | | |
| | | | | |
| | | | | |
| | | | | |
| | | | | |
| | | | | |
| | | | | |
| | | | | |
| | | | | |
| | | | | |

## NOTES & More

## SPECIAL REMINDERS

# Planning Snapshot

## CEREMONY EXPENSE TRACKER

|  | BUDGET | COST | DEPOSIT | BALANCE | DUE DATE |
|---|---|---|---|---|---|
| OFFICIANT GRATUITY |  |  |  |  |  |
| MARRIAGE LICENSE |  |  |  |  |  |
| VENUE COST |  |  |  |  |  |
| FLOWERS |  |  |  |  |  |
| DECORATIONS |  |  |  |  |  |
| OTHER |  |  |  |  |  |

## NOTES & Reminders

### NOTES & REMINDERS

## RECEPTION EXPENSE TRACKER

|  | BUDGET | COST | DEPOSIT | BALANCE | DUE DATE |
|---|---|---|---|---|---|
| VENUE FEE |  |  |  |  |  |
| CATERING/FOOD |  |  |  |  |  |
| BAR/BEVERAGES |  |  |  |  |  |
| CAKE/CUTTING FEE |  |  |  |  |  |
| DECORATIONS |  |  |  |  |  |
| RENTALS/EXTRAS |  |  |  |  |  |
| BARTENDER/STAFF |  |  |  |  |  |

## NOTES & More

### SPECIAL REMINDERS

# Planning Snapshot

## PAPER PRODUCTS EXPENSE TRACKER

|  | BUDGET | COST | DEPOSIT | BALANCE | DUE DATE |
|---|---|---|---|---|---|
| INVITATIONS/CARDS |  |  |  |  |  |
| POSTAGE COSTS |  |  |  |  |  |
| THANK YOU CARDS |  |  |  |  |  |
| PLACE CARDS |  |  |  |  |  |
| GUESTBOOK |  |  |  |  |  |
| OTHER |  |  |  |  |  |

### NOTES & Reminders

NOTES & REMINDERS

## ENTERTAINMENT EXPENSE TRACKER

|  | BUDGET | COST | DEPOSIT | BALANCE | DUE DATE |
|---|---|---|---|---|---|
| BAND/DJ |  |  |  |  |  |
| SOUND SYSTEM RENTAL |  |  |  |  |  |
| VENUE/DANCE RENTAL |  |  |  |  |  |
| GRATUITIES |  |  |  |  |  |
| OTHER: |  |  |  |  |  |
| OTHER: |  |  |  |  |  |
| OTHER: |  |  |  |  |  |

### NOTES & More

SPECIAL REMINDERS

# Planning Snapshot

## WEDDING PARTY ATTIRE EXPENSE TRACKER

|  | BUDGET | COST | DEPOSIT | BALANCE | DUE DATE |
|---|---|---|---|---|---|
| WEDDING DRESS | | | | | |
| TUX RENTALS | | | | | |
| BRIDESMAID DRESSES | | | | | |
| SHOES/HEELS | | | | | |
| VEIL/GARTER/OTHER | | | | | |
| ALTERATION COSTS | | | | | |

### NOTES & Reminders

NOTES & REMINDERS

## TRANSPORTATION EXPENSE TRACKER

|  | BUDGET | COST | DEPOSIT | BALANCE | DUE DATE |
|---|---|---|---|---|---|
| LIMO RENTAL | | | | | |
| VALET PARKING | | | | | |
| VENUE TRANSPORTATION | | | | | |
| AIRPORT TRANSPORTATION | | | | | |
| OTHER: | | | | | |
| OTHER: | | | | | |
| OTHER: | | | | | |

### NOTES & More

SPECIAL REMINDERS

# Planning Snapshot

## FLORIST EXPENSE TRACKER

|  | BUDGET | COST | DEPOSIT | BALANCE | DUE DATE |
|---|---|---|---|---|---|
| BOUQUETS |  |  |  |  |  |
| VENUE DECORATIONS |  |  |  |  |  |
| BOUTONNIERES |  |  |  |  |  |
| VASES/EXTRAS |  |  |  |  |  |
| TABLE DECORATIONS |  |  |  |  |  |
| OTHER: |  |  |  |  |  |

### NOTES & Reminders

NOTES & REMINDERS

## OTHER EXPENSE TRACKER

|  | BUDGET | COST | DEPOSIT | BALANCE | DUE DATE |
|---|---|---|---|---|---|
| PHOTOGRAPHER |  |  |  |  |  |
| VIDEOGRAPHER |  |  |  |  |  |
| CATERER |  |  |  |  |  |
| HAIR/MAKEUP/SALON |  |  |  |  |  |
| WEDDING RINGS |  |  |  |  |  |
| WEDDING PARTY GIFTS |  |  |  |  |  |
| OTHER: |  |  |  |  |  |

### NOTES & More

SPECIAL REMINDERS

# Bride's Planner

## HAIR APPOINTMENT

| SALON NAME | DATE | TIME | BOOKED FOR: | ADDRESS: |
|------------|------|------|-------------|----------|
|  |  |  | ☐ |  |
|  |  |  | ☐ |  |
|  |  |  | ☐ |  |

NOTES

## MAKE UP APPOINTMENT

| SALON NAME | DATE | TIME | BOOKED FOR: | ADDRESS: |
|------------|------|------|-------------|----------|
|  |  |  | ☐ |  |
|  |  |  | ☐ |  |
|  |  |  | ☐ |  |

NOTES

## MANICURE/PEDICURE APPOINTMENT

| SALON NAME | DATE | TIME | BOOKED FOR: | ADDRESS: |
|------------|------|------|-------------|----------|
|  |  |  | ☐ |  |
|  |  |  | ☐ |  |
|  |  |  | ☐ |  |

NOTES

# Groom's Planner

## HAIR APPOINTMENT

| SALON NAME | DATE | TIME | BOOKED FOR: | | ADDRESS: |
|------------|------|------|-------------|---|----------|
| | | | | ☐ | |
| | | | | ☐ | |
| | | | | ☐ | |

**NOTES**

## TUX FITTING APPOINTMENT

| BUSINESS NAME | DATE | TIME | BOOKED FOR: | | ADDRESS: |
|---------------|------|------|-------------|---|----------|
| | | | | ☐ | |
| | | | | ☐ | |

**NOTES**

## OTHER:

| BUSINESS NAME | DATE | TIME | BOOKED FOR: | | ADDRESS: |
|---------------|------|------|-------------|---|----------|
| | | | | ☐ | |
| | | | | ☐ | |
| | | | | ☐ | |

**NOTES**

# Important Dates

| DATE: | DATE: | DATE: | REMINDERS |
|---|---|---|---|
| | | | |
| DATE: | DATE: | DATE: | |
| | | | |
| DATE: | DATE: | DATE: | |
| | | | NOTES |
| DATE: | DATE: | DATE: | |
| | | | |
| DATE: | DATE: | DATE: | |
| | | | |

# Weekly Wedding Planning

WEEK OF: _____

## MONDAY

## TUESDAY

## WEDNESDAY

## THURSDAY

## FRIDAY

## SATURDAY

### WEDDING TO DO LIST

☐ _____
☐ _____
☐ _____
☐ _____
☐ _____
☐ _____
☐ _____
☐ _____
☐ _____
☐ _____
☐ _____
☐ _____
☐ _____
☐ _____
☐ _____

### APPOINTMENTS & MEETINGS

| DATE | TIME | VENDOR | PURPOSE |
|------|------|--------|---------|
|      |      |        |         |
|      |      |        |         |
|      |      |        |         |
|      |      |        |         |
|      |      |        |         |
|      |      |        |         |
|      |      |        |         |
|      |      |        |         |
|      |      |        |         |
|      |      |        |         |
|      |      |        |         |
|      |      |        |         |
|      |      |        |         |
|      |      |        |         |
|      |      |        |         |
|      |      |        |         |
|      |      |        |         |

# Weekly Wedding Planning

WEEK OF: _____

| MONDAY |
| --- |
|  |

| TUESDAY |
| --- |
|  |

| WEDNESDAY |
| --- |
|  |

| THURSDAY |
| --- |
|  |

| FRIDAY |
| --- |
|  |

| SATURDAY |
| --- |
|  |

## WEDDING TO DO LIST

- ☐ _____
- ☐ _____
- ☐ _____
- ☐ _____
- ☐ _____
- ☐ _____
- ☐ _____
- ☐ _____
- ☐ _____
- ☐ _____
- ☐ _____
- ☐ _____
- ☐ _____
- ☐ _____

| APPOINTMENTS & MEETINGS | | | |
| --- | --- | --- | --- |
| DATE | TIME | VENDOR | PURPOSE |
|  |  |  |  |
|  |  |  |  |
|  |  |  |  |
|  |  |  |  |
|  |  |  |  |
|  |  |  |  |
|  |  |  |  |
|  |  |  |  |
|  |  |  |  |
|  |  |  |  |
|  |  |  |  |
|  |  |  |  |
|  |  |  |  |
|  |  |  |  |
|  |  |  |  |
|  |  |  |  |
|  |  |  |  |
|  |  |  |  |
|  |  |  |  |

# Weekly Wedding Planning

WEEK OF: _____

| MONDAY |
| --- |
| |

| TUESDAY |
| --- |
| |

| WEDNESDAY |
| --- |
| |

| THURSDAY |
| --- |
| |

| FRIDAY |
| --- |
| |

| SATURDAY |
| --- |
| |

## WEDDING TO DO LIST

- [ ] _____
- [ ] _____
- [ ] _____
- [ ] _____
- [ ] _____
- [ ] _____
- [ ] _____
- [ ] _____
- [ ] _____
- [ ] _____
- [ ] _____
- [ ] _____
- [ ] _____
- [ ] _____
- [ ] _____
- [ ] _____

## APPOINTMENTS & MEETINGS

| DATE | TIME | VENDOR | PURPOSE |
| --- | --- | --- | --- |
| | | | |
| | | | |
| | | | |
| | | | |
| | | | |
| | | | |
| | | | |
| | | | |
| | | | |
| | | | |
| | | | |
| | | | |
| | | | |
| | | | |
| | | | |
| | | | |
| | | | |
| | | | |

# Weekly Wedding Planning

WEEK OF: _____

| MONDAY |
| --- |
| |

## WEDDING TO DO LIST

- ☐ _____
- ☐ _____
- ☐ _____
- ☐ _____
- ☐ _____
- ☐ _____
- ☐ _____
- ☐ _____
- ☐ _____
- ☐ _____
- ☐ _____
- ☐ _____
- ☐ _____
- ☐ _____
- ☐ _____

| TUESDAY |
| --- |
| |

| WEDNESDAY |
| --- |
| |

| THURSDAY |
| --- |
| |

| APPOINTMENTS & MEETINGS | | | |
| --- | --- | --- | --- |
| DATE | TIME | VENDOR | PURPOSE |
| | | | |
| | | | |
| | | | |
| | | | |
| | | | |
| | | | |
| | | | |
| | | | |
| | | | |
| | | | |
| | | | |
| | | | |
| | | | |
| | | | |
| | | | |
| | | | |

| FRIDAY |
| --- |
| |

| SATURDAY |
| --- |
| |

# Weekly Wedding Planning

WEEK OF: _____

| MONDAY |
| --- |
| |

| TUESDAY |
| --- |
| |

| WEDNESDAY |
| --- |
| |

| THURSDAY |
| --- |
| |

| FRIDAY |
| --- |
| |

| SATURDAY |
| --- |
| |

## WEDDING TO DO LIST

- ☐ _____
- ☐ _____
- ☐ _____
- ☐ _____
- ☐ _____
- ☐ _____
- ☐ _____
- ☐ _____
- ☐ _____
- ☐ _____
- ☐ _____
- ☐ _____
- ☐ _____
- ☐ _____
- ☐ _____
- ☐ _____

## APPOINTMENTS & MEETINGS

| DATE | TIME | VENDOR | PURPOSE |
| --- | --- | --- | --- |
| | | | |
| | | | |
| | | | |
| | | | |
| | | | |
| | | | |
| | | | |
| | | | |
| | | | |
| | | | |
| | | | |
| | | | |
| | | | |
| | | | |
| | | | |
| | | | |
| | | | |
| | | | |

# Weekly Wedding Planning

WEEK OF: _____

## MONDAY

## TUESDAY

## WEDNESDAY

## THURSDAY

## FRIDAY

## SATURDAY

### WEDDING TO DO LIST

- [ ] _____
- [ ] _____
- [ ] _____
- [ ] _____
- [ ] _____
- [ ] _____
- [ ] _____
- [ ] _____
- [ ] _____
- [ ] _____
- [ ] _____
- [ ] _____
- [ ] _____
- [ ] _____
- [ ] _____
- [ ] _____

| APPOINTMENTS & MEETINGS | | | |
|---|---|---|---|
| DATE | TIME | VENDOR | PURPOSE |
| | | | |
| | | | |
| | | | |
| | | | |
| | | | |
| | | | |
| | | | |
| | | | |
| | | | |
| | | | |
| | | | |
| | | | |
| | | | |
| | | | |
| | | | |
| | | | |
| | | | |

# Weekly Wedding Planning

WEEK OF: _____

| MONDAY |
| --- |
| |

| TUESDAY |
| --- |
| |

| WEDNESDAY |
| --- |
| |

| THURSDAY |
| --- |
| |

| FRIDAY |
| --- |
| |

| SATURDAY |
| --- |
| |

### WEDDING TO DO LIST

- ☐ _____
- ☐ _____
- ☐ _____
- ☐ _____
- ☐ _____
- ☐ _____
- ☐ _____
- ☐ _____
- ☐ _____
- ☐ _____
- ☐ _____
- ☐ _____
- ☐ _____
- ☐ _____
- ☐ _____
- ☐ _____

| APPOINTMENTS & MEETINGS | | | |
| --- | --- | --- | --- |
| DATE | TIME | VENDOR | PURPOSE |
| | | | |
| | | | |
| | | | |
| | | | |
| | | | |
| | | | |
| | | | |
| | | | |
| | | | |
| | | | |
| | | | |
| | | | |
| | | | |
| | | | |
| | | | |
| | | | |
| | | | |
| | | | |

# Weekly Wedding Planning

WEEK OF: _____

| MONDAY |
| --- |
| |

| TUESDAY |
| --- |
| |

| WEDNESDAY |
| --- |
| |

| THURSDAY |
| --- |
| |

| FRIDAY |
| --- |
| |

| SATURDAY |
| --- |
| |

## WEDDING TO DO LIST

- ☐ _____
- ☐ _____
- ☐ _____
- ☐ _____
- ☐ _____
- ☐ _____
- ☐ _____
- ☐ _____
- ☐ _____
- ☐ _____
- ☐ _____
- ☐ _____
- ☐ _____
- ☐ _____
- ☐ _____
- ☐ _____
- ☐ _____

## APPOINTMENTS & MEETINGS

| DATE | TIME | VENDOR | PURPOSE |
| --- | --- | --- | --- |
| | | | |
| | | | |
| | | | |
| | | | |
| | | | |
| | | | |
| | | | |
| | | | |
| | | | |
| | | | |
| | | | |
| | | | |
| | | | |
| | | | |
| | | | |
| | | | |
| | | | |
| | | | |
| | | | |

# Weekly Wedding Planning

WEEK OF: _____

| MONDAY |
| --- |
| |

| TUESDAY |
| --- |
| |

| WEDNESDAY |
| --- |
| |

| THURSDAY |
| --- |
| |

| FRIDAY |
| --- |
| |

| SATURDAY |
| --- |
| |

## WEDDING TO DO LIST

☐ _____
☐ _____
☐ _____
☐ _____
☐ _____
☐ _____
☐ _____
☐ _____
☐ _____
☐ _____
☐ _____
☐ _____
☐ _____
☐ _____
☐ _____
☐ _____

## APPOINTMENTS & MEETINGS

| DATE | TIME | VENDOR | PURPOSE |
| --- | --- | --- | --- |
| | | | |
| | | | |
| | | | |
| | | | |
| | | | |
| | | | |
| | | | |
| | | | |
| | | | |
| | | | |
| | | | |
| | | | |
| | | | |
| | | | |
| | | | |
| | | | |
| | | | |

# Weekly Wedding Planning

WEEK OF: _____

## MONDAY

## TUESDAY

## WEDNESDAY

## THURSDAY

## FRIDAY

## SATURDAY

### WEDDING TO DO LIST

- ☐ _____
- ☐ _____
- ☐ _____
- ☐ _____
- ☐ _____
- ☐ _____
- ☐ _____
- ☐ _____
- ☐ _____
- ☐ _____
- ☐ _____
- ☐ _____
- ☐ _____
- ☐ _____
- ☐ _____
- ☐ _____

### APPOINTMENTS & MEETINGS

| DATE | TIME | VENDOR | PURPOSE |
|------|------|--------|---------|
|      |      |        |         |
|      |      |        |         |
|      |      |        |         |
|      |      |        |         |
|      |      |        |         |
|      |      |        |         |
|      |      |        |         |
|      |      |        |         |
|      |      |        |         |
|      |      |        |         |
|      |      |        |         |
|      |      |        |         |
|      |      |        |         |
|      |      |        |         |
|      |      |        |         |
|      |      |        |         |
|      |      |        |         |

# Weekly Wedding Planning

**WEEK OF:** _____

| MONDAY |
| --- |
| |

| TUESDAY |
| --- |
| |

| WEDNESDAY |
| --- |
| |

| THURSDAY |
| --- |
| |

| FRIDAY |
| --- |
| |

| SATURDAY |
| --- |
| |

## WEDDING TO DO LIST

- ☐ _____
- ☐ _____
- ☐ _____
- ☐ _____
- ☐ _____
- ☐ _____
- ☐ _____
- ☐ _____
- ☐ _____
- ☐ _____
- ☐ _____
- ☐ _____
- ☐ _____
- ☐ _____
- ☐ _____
- ☐ _____

### APPOINTMENTS & MEETINGS

| DATE | TIME | VENDOR | PURPOSE |
| --- | --- | --- | --- |
| | | | |
| | | | |
| | | | |
| | | | |
| | | | |
| | | | |
| | | | |
| | | | |
| | | | |
| | | | |
| | | | |
| | | | |
| | | | |
| | | | |
| | | | |
| | | | |
| | | | |
| | | | |

# Weekly Wedding Planning

WEEK OF: _____

| MONDAY |
| --- |
| |

| TUESDAY |
| --- |
| |

| WEDNESDAY |
| --- |
| |

| THURSDAY |
| --- |
| |

| FRIDAY |
| --- |
| |

| SATURDAY |
| --- |
| |

## WEDDING TO DO LIST

☐ _____
☐ _____
☐ _____
☐ _____
☐ _____
☐ _____
☐ _____
☐ _____
☐ _____
☐ _____
☐ _____
☐ _____
☐ _____
☐ _____
☐ _____

| APPOINTMENTS & MEETINGS | | | |
| --- | --- | --- | --- |
| DATE | TIME | VENDOR | PURPOSE |
| | | | |
| | | | |
| | | | |
| | | | |
| | | | |
| | | | |
| | | | |
| | | | |
| | | | |
| | | | |
| | | | |
| | | | |
| | | | |
| | | | |
| | | | |
| | | | |
| | | | |
| | | | |

# Weekly Wedding Planning

WEEK OF: _____

| MONDAY |
| --- |
| |

## WEDDING TO DO LIST

- [ ] _____
- [ ] _____
- [ ] _____
- [ ] _____
- [ ] _____
- [ ] _____
- [ ] _____
- [ ] _____
- [ ] _____
- [ ] _____
- [ ] _____
- [ ] _____
- [ ] _____
- [ ] _____
- [ ] _____
- [ ] _____

| TUESDAY |
| --- |
| |

| WEDNESDAY |
| --- |
| |

| THURSDAY |
| --- |
| |

## APPOINTMENTS & MEETINGS

| DATE | TIME | VENDOR | PURPOSE |
| --- | --- | --- | --- |
| | | | |
| | | | |
| | | | |
| | | | |
| | | | |
| | | | |
| | | | |
| | | | |
| | | | |
| | | | |
| | | | |
| | | | |
| | | | |
| | | | |
| | | | |
| | | | |
| | | | |
| | | | |

| FRIDAY |
| --- |
| |

| SATURDAY |
| --- |
| |

# Weekly Wedding Planning

WEEK OF: _____

## MONDAY

## TUESDAY

## WEDNESDAY

## THURSDAY

## FRIDAY

## SATURDAY

### WEDDING TO DO LIST

☐ _____
☐ _____
☐ _____
☐ _____
☐ _____
☐ _____
☐ _____
☐ _____
☐ _____
☐ _____
☐ _____
☐ _____
☐ _____
☐ _____
☐ _____
☐ _____
☐ _____

### APPOINTMENTS & MEETINGS

| DATE | TIME | VENDOR | PURPOSE |
|------|------|--------|---------|
|      |      |        |         |
|      |      |        |         |
|      |      |        |         |
|      |      |        |         |
|      |      |        |         |
|      |      |        |         |
|      |      |        |         |
|      |      |        |         |
|      |      |        |         |
|      |      |        |         |
|      |      |        |         |
|      |      |        |         |
|      |      |        |         |
|      |      |        |         |
|      |      |        |         |
|      |      |        |         |
|      |      |        |         |
|      |      |        |         |

# Weekly Wedding Planning

WEEK OF: _____

## MONDAY

## TUESDAY

## WEDNESDAY

## THURSDAY

## FRIDAY

## SATURDAY

### WEDDING TO DO LIST

- ☐ _____
- ☐ _____
- ☐ _____
- ☐ _____
- ☐ _____
- ☐ _____
- ☐ _____
- ☐ _____
- ☐ _____
- ☐ _____
- ☐ _____
- ☐ _____
- ☐ _____
- ☐ _____
- ☐ _____
- ☐ _____

### APPOINTMENTS & MEETINGS

| DATE | TIME | VENDOR | PURPOSE |
|------|------|--------|---------|
|      |      |        |         |
|      |      |        |         |
|      |      |        |         |
|      |      |        |         |
|      |      |        |         |
|      |      |        |         |
|      |      |        |         |
|      |      |        |         |
|      |      |        |         |
|      |      |        |         |
|      |      |        |         |
|      |      |        |         |
|      |      |        |         |
|      |      |        |         |
|      |      |        |         |
|      |      |        |         |
|      |      |        |         |
|      |      |        |         |

# Weekly Wedding Planning

WEEK OF: _____

| MONDAY |
| --- |
| |

| TUESDAY |
| --- |
| |

| WEDNESDAY |
| --- |
| |

| THURSDAY |
| --- |
| |

| FRIDAY |
| --- |
| |

| SATURDAY |
| --- |
| |

### WEDDING TO DO LIST

- ☐ _____
- ☐ _____
- ☐ _____
- ☐ _____
- ☐ _____
- ☐ _____
- ☐ _____
- ☐ _____
- ☐ _____
- ☐ _____
- ☐ _____
- ☐ _____
- ☐ _____
- ☐ _____
- ☐ _____

### APPOINTMENTS & MEETINGS

| DATE | TIME | VENDOR | PURPOSE |
| --- | --- | --- | --- |
| | | | |
| | | | |
| | | | |
| | | | |
| | | | |
| | | | |
| | | | |
| | | | |
| | | | |
| | | | |
| | | | |
| | | | |
| | | | |
| | | | |
| | | | |
| | | | |
| | | | |
| | | | |

# Weekly Wedding Planning

WEEK OF: _____

| MONDAY |
| --- |
|  |

WEDDING TO DO LIST

- ☐ _____
- ☐ _____
- ☐ _____
- ☐ _____
- ☐ _____
- ☐ _____
- ☐ _____
- ☐ _____
- ☐ _____
- ☐ _____
- ☐ _____
- ☐ _____
- ☐ _____
- ☐ _____
- ☐ _____
- ☐ _____

| TUESDAY |
| --- |
|  |

| WEDNESDAY |
| --- |
|  |

| THURSDAY |
| --- |
|  |

| APPOINTMENTS & MEETINGS | | | |
| --- | --- | --- | --- |
| DATE | TIME | VENDOR | PURPOSE |
|  |  |  |  |
|  |  |  |  |
|  |  |  |  |
|  |  |  |  |
|  |  |  |  |
|  |  |  |  |
|  |  |  |  |
|  |  |  |  |
|  |  |  |  |
|  |  |  |  |
|  |  |  |  |
|  |  |  |  |
|  |  |  |  |
|  |  |  |  |
|  |  |  |  |
|  |  |  |  |
|  |  |  |  |
|  |  |  |  |

| FRIDAY |
| --- |
|  |

| SATURDAY |
| --- |
|  |

# Weekly Wedding Planning

WEEK OF: _____

### MONDAY

### TUESDAY

### WEDNESDAY

### THURSDAY

### FRIDAY

### SATURDAY

## WEDDING TO DO LIST

☐ _____
☐ _____
☐ _____
☐ _____
☐ _____
☐ _____
☐ _____
☐ _____
☐ _____
☐ _____
☐ _____
☐ _____
☐ _____
☐ _____
☐ _____
☐ _____
☐ _____

| APPOINTMENTS & MEETINGS | | | |
|---|---|---|---|
| DATE | TIME | VENDOR | PURPOSE |
| | | | |
| | | | |
| | | | |
| | | | |
| | | | |
| | | | |
| | | | |
| | | | |
| | | | |
| | | | |
| | | | |
| | | | |
| | | | |
| | | | |
| | | | |
| | | | |
| | | | |
| | | | |
| | | | |

# Weekly Wedding Planning

WEEK OF: _____

| MONDAY |
| --- |
| |

| TUESDAY |
| --- |
| |

| WEDNESDAY |
| --- |
| |

| THURSDAY |
| --- |
| |

| FRIDAY |
| --- |
| |

| SATURDAY |
| --- |
| |

## WEDDING TO DO LIST

☐ _____
☐ _____
☐ _____
☐ _____
☐ _____
☐ _____
☐ _____
☐ _____
☐ _____
☐ _____
☐ _____
☐ _____
☐ _____
☐ _____
☐ _____
☐ _____

## APPOINTMENTS & MEETINGS

| DATE | TIME | VENDOR | PURPOSE |
| --- | --- | --- | --- |
| | | | |
| | | | |
| | | | |
| | | | |
| | | | |
| | | | |
| | | | |
| | | | |
| | | | |
| | | | |
| | | | |
| | | | |
| | | | |
| | | | |
| | | | |
| | | | |
| | | | |
| | | | |

# Wedding Planner

## - PLANNING GUIDELINE -

| | | |
|---|---|---|
| FINALIZE GUEST LIST | ORDER BRIDESMAIDS DRESSES | BOOK FLORIST |
| ORDER INVITATIONS | RESERVE TUXEDOS | BOOK DJ/ENTERTAINMENT |
| PLAN YOUR RECEPTION | ARRANGE TRANSPORTATION | BOOK CATERER |
| BOOK PHOTOGRAPHER | BOOK WEDDING VENUE | CHOOSE WEDDING CAKE |
| BOOK VIDEOGRAPHER | BOOK RECEPTION VENUE | BOOK OFFICIANT |
| CHOOSE WEDDING GOWN | PLAN HONEYMOON | BOOK ROOMS FOR GUESTS |

## Things To Do          Status

## TOP PRIORITIES

## NOTES & IDEAS

## APPOINTMENTS & REMINDERS

# Wedding Planner

## - PLANNING GUIDELINE -

- ORDER THANK YOU NOTES
- REVIEW RECEPTION DETAILS
- MAKE APPT FOR FITTING
- CONFIRM BRIDAL DRESSES
- OBTAIN MARRIAGE LICENSE
- BOOK HAIR STYLIST

- BOOK NAIL SALON
- CONFIRM MUSIC SELECTION
- WRITE VOWS
- PLAN BRIDAL SHOWER
- PLAN REHEARSAL
- BOOK REHEARSAL DINNER

- SHOP FOR WEDDING RINGS
- PLAN DECORATIONS
- CHOOSE BOUQUET TYPE
- FINALIZE GUEST LIST
- UPDATE PASSPORTS
- CONFIRM HOTEL ROOMS

| Things To Do | Status |
|---|---|
| | |
| | |
| | |
| | |
| | |
| | |
| | |
| | |
| | |
| | |
| | |
| | |
| | |
| | |
| | |
| | |
| | |
| | |
| | |
| | |
| | |
| | |
| | |

### TOP PRIORITIES

### NOTES & IDEAS

### APPOINTMENTS & REMINDERS

# Wedding Planner

## - PLANNING GUIDELINE -

| | | |
|---|---|---|
| MAIL OUT INVITATIONS | FINALIZE HONEYMOON PLANS | CONFIRM CATERER |
| MEET WITH OFFICIANT | ATTEND FIRST DRESS FITTING | FINALIZE RING FITTING |
| BUY WEDDING FAVORS | FINALIZE VOWS | CONFIRM FLOWERS |
| BUY WEDDING PARTY GIFTS | FINALIZE RECEPTION MENU | CONFIRM BAND |
| PURCHASE SHOES | KEEP TRACK OF RSVPS | SHOP FOR HONEYMOON |
| FINALIZE THANK YOU CARDS | BOOK PHOTO SESSION | BUY GARTER BELT |

## Things To Do                Status

## TOP PRIORITIES

## NOTES & IDEAS

## APPOINTMENTS & REMINDERS

# Wedding Planner

## - PLANNING GUIDELINE -

- CHOOSE YOUR MC
- REQUEST SPECIAL TOASTS
- ARRANGE TRANSPORTATION
- CHOOSE YOUR HAIR STYLE
- CHOOSE YOUR NAIL COLOR
- ATTEND BRIDAL SHOWER

- CONFIRM CAKE CHOICES
- CONFIRM MENU (FINAL)
- CONFIRM SEATING
- CONFIRM VIDEOGRAPHER
- ARRANGE LEGAL DOCS
- FINALIZE WEDDING DUTIES

- CONFIRM BRIDESMAID DRESSES
- MEET WITH DJ/MC
- FINAL DRESS FITTING
- WRAP WEDDIING PARTY GIFTS
- CONFIRM FINAL GUEST COUNT
- CREATE WEDDING SCHEDULE

| Things To Do | Status |
|---|---|
| | |
| | |
| | |
| | |
| | |
| | |
| | |
| | |
| | |
| | |
| | |
| | |
| | |
| | |
| | |
| | |
| | |
| | |
| | |
| | |
| | |
| | |
| | |

### TOP PRIORITIES

### NOTES & IDEAS

### APPOINTMENTS & REMINDERS

# Wedding Planner

## - PLANNING GUIDELINE -

PAYMENT TO VENDORS

PACK FOR HONEYMOON

CONFIRM HOTEL RESERVATION

GIVE SCHEDULE TO PARTY

DELIVER LICENSE TO OFFICIANT

CONFIRM WITH VENDORS

PICK UP WEDDING DRESS

PICK UP TUXEDOS

GIVE MUSIC LIST TO DJ/BAND

CONFIRM SHOES/HEELS FIT

CONFIRM TRANSPORTATION

MONEY FOR GRATUITIES

COMPLETE MAKE UP TRIAL

CONFIRM RINGS FIT

CONFIRM TRAVEL PLANS

CONFIRM HOTELS FOR GUESTS

OTHER: _____

OTHER: _____

| Things To Do | Status |
|---|---|
|  |  |
|  |  |
|  |  |
|  |  |
|  |  |
|  |  |
|  |  |
|  |  |
|  |  |
|  |  |
|  |  |
|  |  |
|  |  |
|  |  |
|  |  |
|  |  |
|  |  |
|  |  |
|  |  |
|  |  |
|  |  |
|  |  |
|  |  |
|  |  |
|  |  |
|  |  |
|  |  |

### TOP PRIORITIES

### NOTES & IDEAS

### APPOINTMENTS & REMINDERS

# Wedding Planner

## - PLANNING GUIDELINE -

ATTEND REHEARSAL DINNER

FINISH HONEYMOON PACKING

GREET OUT OF TOWN GUESTS

GET MANICURE/PEDICURE

CHECK ON WEDDING VENUE

CHECK WEATHER TO PREPARE

GIVE GIFTS TO WEDDING PARTY

CONFIRM RINGS FIT

GET A GOOD NIGHT'S SLEEP

| Things To Do | Status |
|---|---|
|  |  |
|  |  |
|  |  |
|  |  |
|  |  |
|  |  |
|  |  |
|  |  |
|  |  |
|  |  |
|  |  |
|  |  |
|  |  |
|  |  |

### TOP PRIORITIES

### NOTES & IDEAS

### APPOINTMENTS & REMINDERS

# Your Special Day!

Day of WEDDING

GET YOUR HAIR DONE

GET YOUR MAKE UP DONE

HAVE A LIGHT BREAKFAST

MEET WITH BRIDAL PARTY

GIVE RINGS TO BEST MAN

ENJOY YOUR SPECIAL DAY!

MR ♡ MRS

# Wedding Attire Planner

| WEDDING ATTIRE EXPENSE TRACKER | | | |
|---|---|---|---|
| ITEM/PURCHASE | STATUS ✓ | DATE PAID | TOTAL COST |
|  |  |  |  |
|  |  |  |  |
|  |  |  |  |
|  |  |  |  |
|  |  |  |  |

| NOTES & REMINDERS | |
|---|---|
|  | **TOTAL COST:** |

Notes:

WEDDING ATTIRE DETAILS

# Venue Planner

## VENUE EXPENSE TRACKER

| ITEM/PURCHASE | STATUS ✓ | DATE PAID | TOTAL COST |
|---|---|---|---|
|  |  |  |  |
|  |  |  |  |
|  |  |  |  |
|  |  |  |  |
|  |  |  |  |

**NOTES & REMINDERS**

**TOTAL COST:**

Notes:

VENUE PLANNING DETAILS

# Catering Planner

| CATERING EXPENSE TRACKER | | | |
|---|---|---|---|
| ITEM/PURCHASE | STATUS ✓ | DATE PAID | TOTAL COST |
| | | | |
| | | | |
| | | | |
| | | | |
| | | | |

| NOTES & REMINDERS | |
|---|---|
| | **TOTAL COST:** |

Notes:

CATERING PLANNER DETAILS

# Entertainment Planner

## ENTERTAINMENT EXPENSE TRACKER

| ITEM/PURCHASE | STATUS ✓ | DATE PAID | TOTAL COST |
|---|---|---|---|
| | | | |
| | | | |
| | | | |
| | | | |
| | | | |

NOTES & REMINDERS

TOTAL COST:

Notes:

Love

ENTERTAINMENT DETAILS

# Videographer Planner

| VIDEOGRAPHER EXPENSE TRACKER | | | |
|---|---|---|---|
| ITEM/PURCHASE | STATUS ✓ | DATE PAID | TOTAL COST |
| | | | |
| | | | |
| | | | |
| | | | |
| | | | |

| NOTES & REMINDERS | |
|---|---|
| | **TOTAL COST:** |

*Notes:*

VIDEOGRAPHER DETAILS

# Photographer Planner

| PHOTOGRAPHER EXPENSE TRACKER | | | |
|---|---|---|---|
| ITEM/PURCHASE | STATUS ✓ | DATE PAID | TOTAL COST |
|  |  |  |  |
|  |  |  |  |
|  |  |  |  |
|  |  |  |  |
|  |  |  |  |

NOTES & REMINDERS

**TOTAL COST:**

Notes:

PHOTOGRAPHER DETAILS

# Florist Planner

| FLORIST EXPENSE TRACKER | | | |
|---|---|---|---|
| ITEM/PURCHASE | STATUS ✓ | DATE PAID | TOTAL COST |
|  |  |  |  |
|  |  |  |  |
|  |  |  |  |
|  |  |  |  |
|  |  |  |  |

NOTES & REMINDERS

TOTAL COST:

Notes:

FLORIST PLANNING DETAILS

# Extra Wedding Costs

| MISC WEDDING EXPENSE TRACKER | | | |
|---|---|---|---|
| ITEM/PURCHASE | STATUS ✓ | DATE PAID | TOTAL COST |
| | | | |
| | | | |
| | | | |
| | | | |
| | | | |

| NOTES & REMINDERS | |
|---|---|
| | **TOTAL COST:** |

Notes:

MISC WEDDING DETAILS

# Bachelorette Party Planner

## EVENT DETAILS

DATE

TIME

VENUE

THEME

HOST

OTHER

| TIME | SCHEDULE OF EVENTS |
|------|--------------------|
|      |                    |
|      |                    |
|      |                    |
|      |                    |
|      |                    |
|      |                    |
|      |                    |
|      |                    |
|      |                    |
|      |                    |
|      |                    |
|      |                    |
|      |                    |
|      |                    |
|      |                    |

## NOTES & REMINDERS

*love*

## GUEST LIST

| FIRST NAME | LAST NAME | R |
|------------|-----------|---|
|            |           |   |
|            |           |   |
|            |           |   |
|            |           |   |
|            |           |   |
|            |           |   |
|            |           |   |
|            |           |   |
|            |           |   |
|            |           |   |
|            |           |   |
|            |           |   |
|            |           |   |
|            |           |   |
|            |           |   |
|            |           |   |
|            |           |   |

## SUPPLIES & SHOPPING LIST

- [ ] 
- [ ] 
- [ ] 
- [ ] 
- [ ] 
- [ ] 
- [ ] 
- [ ] 
- [ ] 
- [ ] 
- [ ] 
- [ ] 
- [ ] 
- [ ] 
- [ ] 
- [ ]

# Bachelor Party Planner

## EVENT DETAILS

DATE

TIME

VENUE

THEME

HOST

OTHER

| TIME | SCHEDULE OF EVENTS |
|------|--------------------|
|      |                    |
|      |                    |
|      |                    |
|      |                    |
|      |                    |
|      |                    |
|      |                    |
|      |                    |
|      |                    |
|      |                    |
|      |                    |
|      |                    |
|      |                    |
|      |                    |
|      |                    |
|      |                    |
|      |                    |

## NOTES & REMINDERS

*love*

## GUEST LIST

| FIRST NAME | LAST NAME | R |
|------------|-----------|---|
|            |           |   |
|            |           |   |
|            |           |   |
|            |           |   |
|            |           |   |
|            |           |   |
|            |           |   |
|            |           |   |
|            |           |   |
|            |           |   |
|            |           |   |
|            |           |   |
|            |           |   |
|            |           |   |
|            |           |   |
|            |           |   |

## SUPPLIES & SHOPPING LIST

- [ ] 
- [ ] 
- [ ] 
- [ ] 
- [ ] 
- [ ] 
- [ ] 
- [ ] 
- [ ] 
- [ ] 
- [ ] 
- [ ] 
- [ ] 
- [ ] 
- [ ] 
- [ ] 
- [ ] 
- [ ]

# Reception Planner

**MEAL PLANNER IDEAS**

**HORS D'OEUVRES**

**1st COURSE:**

**3rd COURSE:**

**2nd COURSE:**

**4th COURSE:**

**MEAL PLANNING NOTES**

# Wedding Planning Notes

# Wedding Planning Notes

**IDEAS & REMINDERS**

# Wedding Planning Notes

**IDEAS & REMINDERS**

_____
_____
_____
_____
_____
_____
_____
_____
_____
_____
_____
_____
_____
_____
_____
_____
_____
_____
_____
_____
_____
_____
_____
_____

# Wedding Planning Notes

**IDEAS & REMINDERS**

# Wedding to do List

PLANNING FOR THE BIG DAY

# Wedding to do List

# Wedding to do List

**PLANNING FOR THE BIG DAY**

# Wedding Prompts

What wedding preparations have been the hardest? How is it progressing?

_____
_____
_____
_____
_____
_____
_____
_____
_____
_____
_____

What is the one thing you're looking forward to most?

_____
_____
_____
_____
_____
_____
_____
_____
_____
_____
_____
_____

# Wedding Prompts

What do you want people to remember most about your wedding?

_____

_____

_____

_____

_____

_____

_____

_____

_____

_____

_____

_____

Write about all your dreams and hopes for this wedding.

_____

_____

_____

_____

_____

_____

_____

_____

_____

_____

_____

_____

# Wedding Prompts

Be honest: are you being too controlling of the wedding preparations?

_____
_____
_____
_____
_____
_____
_____
_____
_____
_____
_____
_____

What are the perfect wedding vows?

_____
_____
_____
_____
_____
_____
_____
_____
_____
_____
_____

# Wedding Prompts

Have you been able to stay within your budget with the wedding planning?

_____
_____
_____
_____
_____
_____
_____
_____
_____
_____
_____
_____

Is the wedding more for you or family members?

_____
_____
_____
_____
_____
_____
_____
_____
_____
_____
_____
_____

# Wedding Prompts
JOURNALING

Describe the perfect honeymoon.

_____
_____
_____
_____
_____
_____
_____
_____
_____
_____
_____
_____

If you could change anything about the wedding, what would it be?

_____
_____
_____
_____
_____
_____
_____
_____
_____
_____
_____

# Wedding Guest List

| NAME | ADDRESS | PHONE # | # IN PARTY | RSVP: ✓ |
|------|---------|---------|------------|---------|
|      |         |         |            |         |
|      |         |         |            |         |
|      |         |         |            |         |
|      |         |         |            |         |
|      |         |         |            |         |
|      |         |         |            |         |
|      |         |         |            |         |
|      |         |         |            |         |
|      |         |         |            |         |
|      |         |         |            |         |
|      |         |         |            |         |
|      |         |         |            |         |
|      |         |         |            |         |
|      |         |         |            |         |
|      |         |         |            |         |
|      |         |         |            |         |
|      |         |         |            |         |
|      |         |         |            |         |

# Wedding Guest List

| NAME | ADDRESS | PHONE # | # IN PARTY | RSVP: ✓ |
|------|---------|---------|------------|---------|
|      |         |         |            |         |
|      |         |         |            |         |
|      |         |         |            |         |
|      |         |         |            |         |
|      |         |         |            |         |
|      |         |         |            |         |
|      |         |         |            |         |
|      |         |         |            |         |
|      |         |         |            |         |
|      |         |         |            |         |
|      |         |         |            |         |
|      |         |         |            |         |
|      |         |         |            |         |
|      |         |         |            |         |
|      |         |         |            |         |
|      |         |         |            |         |
|      |         |         |            |         |
|      |         |         |            |         |

# Wedding Guest List

| NAME | ADDRESS | PHONE # | # IN PARTY | RSVP: ✓ |
|------|---------|---------|------------|---------|
|  |  |  |  |  |
|  |  |  |  |  |
|  |  |  |  |  |
|  |  |  |  |  |
|  |  |  |  |  |
|  |  |  |  |  |
|  |  |  |  |  |
|  |  |  |  |  |
|  |  |  |  |  |
|  |  |  |  |  |
|  |  |  |  |  |
|  |  |  |  |  |
|  |  |  |  |  |
|  |  |  |  |  |
|  |  |  |  |  |
|  |  |  |  |  |
|  |  |  |  |  |
|  |  |  |  |  |
|  |  |  |  |  |

# Wedding Guest List

| NAME | ADDRESS | PHONE # | # IN PARTY | RSVP: ✓ |
|------|---------|---------|------------|---------|
|      |         |         |            |         |
|      |         |         |            |         |
|      |         |         |            |         |
|      |         |         |            |         |
|      |         |         |            |         |
|      |         |         |            |         |
|      |         |         |            |         |
|      |         |         |            |         |
|      |         |         |            |         |
|      |         |         |            |         |
|      |         |         |            |         |
|      |         |         |            |         |
|      |         |         |            |         |
|      |         |         |            |         |
|      |         |         |            |         |

# Wedding Guest List

| NAME | ADDRESS | PHONE # | # IN PARTY | RSVP: ✓ |
|------|---------|---------|------------|---------|
|      |         |         |            |         |
|      |         |         |            |         |
|      |         |         |            |         |
|      |         |         |            |         |
|      |         |         |            |         |
|      |         |         |            |         |
|      |         |         |            |         |
|      |         |         |            |         |
|      |         |         |            |         |
|      |         |         |            |         |
|      |         |         |            |         |
|      |         |         |            |         |
|      |         |         |            |         |
|      |         |         |            |         |
|      |         |         |            |         |
|      |         |         |            |         |
|      |         |         |            |         |
|      |         |         |            |         |

# Wedding Guest List

| NAME | ADDRESS | PHONE # | # IN PARTY | RSVP: ✓ |
|------|---------|---------|-----------|---------|
|      |         |         |           |         |
|      |         |         |           |         |
|      |         |         |           |         |
|      |         |         |           |         |
|      |         |         |           |         |
|      |         |         |           |         |
|      |         |         |           |         |
|      |         |         |           |         |
|      |         |         |           |         |
|      |         |         |           |         |
|      |         |         |           |         |
|      |         |         |           |         |
|      |         |         |           |         |
|      |         |         |           |         |
|      |         |         |           |         |
|      |         |         |           |         |
|      |         |         |           |         |
|      |         |         |           |         |

# Wedding Guest List

| NAME | ADDRESS | PHONE # | # IN PARTY | RSVP: ✓ |
|------|---------|---------|------------|---------|
|      |         |         |            |         |
|      |         |         |            |         |
|      |         |         |            |         |
|      |         |         |            |         |
|      |         |         |            |         |
|      |         |         |            |         |
|      |         |         |            |         |
|      |         |         |            |         |
|      |         |         |            |         |
|      |         |         |            |         |
|      |         |         |            |         |
|      |         |         |            |         |
|      |         |         |            |         |
|      |         |         |            |         |
|      |         |         |            |         |
|      |         |         |            |         |
|      |         |         |            |         |
|      |         |         |            |         |

# Wedding Guest List

| NAME | ADDRESS | PHONE # | # IN PARTY | RSVP: ✓ |
|------|---------|---------|------------|---------|
|  |  |  |  |  |
|  |  |  |  |  |
|  |  |  |  |  |
|  |  |  |  |  |
|  |  |  |  |  |
|  |  |  |  |  |
|  |  |  |  |  |
|  |  |  |  |  |
|  |  |  |  |  |
|  |  |  |  |  |
|  |  |  |  |  |
|  |  |  |  |  |
|  |  |  |  |  |
|  |  |  |  |  |
|  |  |  |  |  |
|  |  |  |  |  |
|  |  |  |  |  |

# Wedding Guest List

| NAME | ADDRESS | PHONE # | # IN PARTY | RSVP: ✓ |
|------|---------|---------|------------|---------|
|      |         |         |            |         |
|      |         |         |            |         |
|      |         |         |            |         |
|      |         |         |            |         |
|      |         |         |            |         |
|      |         |         |            |         |
|      |         |         |            |         |
|      |         |         |            |         |
|      |         |         |            |         |
|      |         |         |            |         |
|      |         |         |            |         |
|      |         |         |            |         |
|      |         |         |            |         |
|      |         |         |            |         |
|      |         |         |            |         |
|      |         |         |            |         |
|      |         |         |            |         |
|      |         |         |            |         |

# Wedding Guest List

| NAME | ADDRESS | PHONE # | # IN PARTY | RSVP: ✓ |
|------|---------|---------|------------|---------|
|  |  |  |  |  |
|  |  |  |  |  |
|  |  |  |  |  |
|  |  |  |  |  |
|  |  |  |  |  |
|  |  |  |  |  |
|  |  |  |  |  |
|  |  |  |  |  |
|  |  |  |  |  |
|  |  |  |  |  |
|  |  |  |  |  |
|  |  |  |  |  |
|  |  |  |  |  |
|  |  |  |  |  |
|  |  |  |  |  |
|  |  |  |  |  |
|  |  |  |  |  |
|  |  |  |  |  |

# Wedding Seating Chart

Table #

Table #

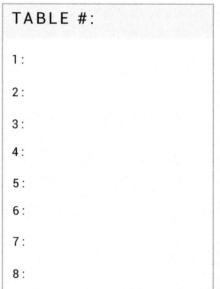

*love*

| TABLE #: |
| --- |
| 1 : |
| 2 : |
| 3 : |
| 4 : |
| 5 : |
| 6 : |
| 7 : |
| 8 : |

| TABLE #: |
| --- |
| 1 : |
| 2 : |
| 3 : |
| 4 : |
| 5 : |
| 6 : |
| 7 : |
| 8 : |

# Wedding Seating Chart

Table #

*love*

Table #

# Wedding Seating Chart

_Table #_

### TABLE #:

1:

2:

3:

4:

5:

6:

7:

8:

_Table #_

### TABLE #:

1:

2:

3:

4:

5:

6:

7:

8:

# Wedding Seating Chart

Table #

TABLE #:

1:

2:

3:

4:

5:

6:

7:

8:

Table #

TABLE #:

1:

2:

3:

4:

5:

6:

7:

8:

# Wedding Seating Chart

Table #

Table #

TABLE #:

1:

2:

3:

4:

5:

6:

7:

8:

TABLE #:

1:

2:

3:

4:

5:

6:

7:

8:

# Wedding Seating Chart

## Table #

| TABLE #: |
| --- |
| 1 : |
| 2 : |
| 3 : |
| 4 : |
| 5 : |
| 6 : |
| 7 : |
| 8 : |

## Table #

| TABLE #: |
| --- |
| 1 : |
| 2 : |
| 3 : |
| 4 : |
| 5 : |
| 6 : |
| 7 : |
| 8 : |

# Wedding Seating Chart

Table #

| TABLE #: |
|---|
| 1: |
| 2: |
| 3: |
| 4: |
| 5: |
| 6: |
| 7: |
| 8: |

Table #

| TABLE #: |
|---|
| 1: |
| 2: |
| 3: |
| 4: |
| 5: |
| 6: |
| 7: |
| 8: |

# Wedding Seating Chart

Table #

TABLE #:

1:

2:

3:

4:

5:

6:

7:

8:

Table #

TABLE #:

1:

2:

3:

4:

5:

6:

7:

8:

# Wedding Seating Chart

Table #

TABLE #:

1:

2:

3:

4:

5:

6:

7:

8:

Table #

TABLE #:

1:

2:

3:

4:

5:

6:

7:

8:

# Wedding Seating Chart

Table #

TABLE #:

1:

2:

3:

4:

5:

6:

7:

8:

Table #

TABLE #:

1:

2:

3:

4:

5:

6:

7:

8:

# Wedding Seating Chart

Table #

Table #

TABLE #:

1:

2:

3:

4:

5:

6:

7:

8:

TABLE #:

1:

2:

3:

4:

5:

6:

7:

8:

# Wedding Seating Chart

Table #

TABLE #:

1:

2:

3:

4:

5:

6:

7:

8:

Table #

TABLE #:

1:

2:

3:

4:

5:

6:

7:

8:

# Wedding Seating Chart

Table #

### TABLE #:

1:

2:

3:

4:

5:

6:

7:

8:

Table #

### TABLE #:

1:

2:

3:

4:

5:

6:

7:

8:

# Wedding Seating Chart

*Table #*

**TABLE #:**

1 :

2 :

3 :

4 :

5 :

6 :

7 :

8 :

*Table #*

**TABLE #:**

1 :

2 :

3 :

4 :

5 :

6 :

7 :

8 :

# Wedding Seating Chart

*Table #*

TABLE #:

1:

2:

3:

4:

5:

6:

7:

8:

*Table #*

TABLE #:

1:

2:

3:

4:

5:

6:

7:

8:

# Wedding Seating Chart

Table #

TABLE #:

1:

2:

3:

4:

5:

6:

7:

8:

Table #

TABLE #:

1:

2:

3:

4:

5:

6:

7:

8:

# Wedding Seating Chart

Table #

### TABLE #:

1:

2:

3:

4:

5:

6:

7:

8:

Table #

### TABLE #:

1:

2:

3:

4:

5:

6:

7:

8:

# Wedding Seating Chart

Table #

TABLE #:

1:

2:

3:

4:

5:

6:

7:

8:

Table #

TABLE #:

1:

2:

3:

4:

5:

6:

7:

8:

# Wedding Seating Chart

Table #

## TABLE #:

1:

2:

3:

4:

5:

6:

7:

8:

Table #

## TABLE #:

1:

2:

3:

4:

5:

6:

7:

8:

# Wedding Seating Chart

Table #

TABLE #:

1:

2:

3:

4:

5:

6:

7:

8:

Table #

TABLE #:

1:

2:

3:

4:

5:

6:

7:

8:

# Wedding Seating Chart

Table #

Table #

**TABLE #:**

1:

2:

3:

4:

5:

6:

7:

8:

**TABLE #:**

1:

2:

3:

4:

5:

6:

7:

8:

# Wedding Seating Chart

Table #

TABLE #:

1:

2:

3:

4:

5:

6:

7:

8:

Table #

TABLE #:

1:

2:

3:

4:

5:

6:

7:

8:

# Wedding Seating Chart

Table #

Table #

TABLE #:

1:

2:

3:

4:

5:

6:

7:

8:

TABLE #:

1:

2:

3:

4:

5:

6:

7:

8:

# Wedding Seating Chart

*Table #*

**TABLE #:**

1 :

2 :

3 :

4 :

5 :

6 :

7 :

8 :

*Table #*

**TABLE #:**

1 :

2 :

3 :

4 :

5 :

6 :

7 :

8 :

# Wedding Seating Chart

Table #

| TABLE #: |
| --- |
| 1 : |
| 2 : |
| 3 : |
| 4 : |
| 5 : |
| 6 : |
| 7 : |
| 8 : |

Table #

| TABLE #: |
| --- |
| 1 : |
| 2 : |
| 3 : |
| 4 : |
| 5 : |
| 6 : |
| 7 : |
| 8 : |

# Wedding Seating Chart

Table #

TABLE #:

1:

2:

3:

4:

5:

6:

7:

8:

Table #

TABLE #:

1:

2:

3:

4:

5:

6:

7:

8:

# Wedding Seating Chart

Table #

TABLE #:

| 1: | 2: | 3: | 4: | 5: | 6: | 7: | 8: |
|----|----|----|----|----|----|----|----|
| 9: | 10: | 11: | 12: | 13: | 14: | 15: | 16: |

Table #

TABLE #:

| 1: | 2: | 3: | 4: | 5: | 6: | 7: | 8: |
|----|----|----|----|----|----|----|----|
| 9: | 10: | 11: | 12: | 13: | 14: | 15: | 16: |

# Wedding Seating Chart

## Table #

## TABLE #:

| 1: | 2: | 3: | 4: | 5: | 6: | 7: | 8: |
|---|---|---|---|---|---|---|---|
| 9: | 10: | 11: | 12: | 13: | 14: | 15: | 16: |

## Table #

## TABLE #:

| 1: | 2: | 3: | 4: | 5: | 6: | 7: | 8: |
|---|---|---|---|---|---|---|---|
| 9: | 10: | 11: | 12: | 13: | 14: | 15: | 16: |

# Wedding Seating Chart

Table #

TABLE #:

| 1: | 2: | 3: | 4: | 5: | 6: | 7: | 8: |
|---|---|---|---|---|---|---|---|
| 9: | 10: | 11: | 12: | 13: | 14: | 15: | 16: |

Table #

TABLE #:

| 1: | 2: | 3: | 4: | 5: | 6: | 7: | 8: |
|---|---|---|---|---|---|---|---|
| 9: | 10: | 11: | 12: | 13: | 14: | 15: | 16: |

# Wedding Seating Chart

Table #

TABLE #:

| 1: | 2: | 3: | 4: | 5: | 6: | 7: | 8: |
|----|----|----|----|----|----|----|----|
| 9: | 10: | 11: | 12: | 13: | 14: | 15: | 16: |

Table #

TABLE #:

| 1: | 2: | 3: | 4: | 5: | 6: | 7: | 8: |
|----|----|----|----|----|----|----|----|
| 9: | 10: | 11: | 12: | 13: | 14: | 15: | 16: |

# Wedding Seating Chart

Table #

TABLE #:

| 1: | 2: | 3: | 4: | 5: | 6: | 7: | 8: |
|----|----|----|----|----|----|----|----|
| 9: | 10: | 11: | 12: | 13: | 14: | 15: | 16: |

Table #

TABLE #:

| 1: | 2: | 3: | 4: | 5: | 6: | 7: | 8: |
|----|----|----|----|----|----|----|----|
| 9: | 10: | 11: | 12: | 13: | 14: | 15: | 16: |

# Wedding Seating Chart

Table #

TABLE #:

| 1: | 2: | 3: | 4: | 5: | 6: | 7: | 8: |
|---|---|---|---|---|---|---|---|
| 9: | 10: | 11: | 12: | 13: | 14: | 15: | 16: |

Table #

TABLE #:

| 1: | 2: | 3: | 4: | 5: | 6: | 7: | 8: |
|---|---|---|---|---|---|---|---|
| 9: | 10: | 11: | 12: | 13: | 14: | 15: | 16: |

# Wedding Seating Chart

Table #

TABLE #:

| 1: | 2: | 3: | 4: | 5: | 6: | 7: | 8: |
|---|---|---|---|---|---|---|---|
| 9: | 10: | 11: | 12: | 13: | 14: | 15: | 16: |

Table #

TABLE #:

| 1: | 2: | 3: | 4: | 5: | 6: | 7: | 8: |
|---|---|---|---|---|---|---|---|
| 9: | 10: | 11: | 12: | 13: | 14: | 15: | 16: |

# Wedding Seating Chart

## Table #

---

**TABLE #:**

| 1: | 2: | 3: | 4: | 5: | 6: | 7: | 8: |
|----|----|----|----|----|----|----|----|
| 9: | 10: | 11: | 12: | 13: | 14: | 15: | 16: |

---

## Table #

---

**TABLE #:**

| 1: | 2: | 3: | 4: | 5: | 6: | 7: | 8: |
|----|----|----|----|----|----|----|----|
| 9: | 10: | 11: | 12: | 13: | 14: | 15: | 16: |

# Wedding Seating Chart

## Table #

## TABLE #:

| 1: | 2: | 3: | 4: | 5: | 6: | 7: | 8: |
|---|---|---|---|---|---|---|---|
| 9: | 10: | 11: | 12: | 13: | 14: | 15: | 16: |

## Table #

## TABLE #:

| 1: | 2: | 3: | 4: | 5: | 6: | 7: | 8: |
|---|---|---|---|---|---|---|---|
| 9: | 10: | 11: | 12: | 13: | 14: | 15: | 16: |

# Wedding Planning Notes

**IDEAS & REMINDERS**

# Wedding to do List

PLANNING FOR THE BIG DAY

# Wedding Planning Notes

**IDEAS & REMINDERS**

# Wedding to do List

PLANNING FOR THE BIG DAY

# Wedding Planning Notes

**IDEAS & REMINDERS**

# Wedding to do List

**PLANNING FOR THE BIG DAY**

Made in United States
North Haven, CT
04 February 2022

15698045R10063